卞尺丹几乙し丹卞と

Translated Language Learning

Die Nachtigall und die Rose

The Nightingale and The Rose

Oscar Wilde

Deutsch / English

Copyright © 2023 Tranzlaty
All rights reserved
ISBN: 978-1-83566-001-0

Original text by Oscar Wilde
The Nightingale and the Rose
Written in 1888 in English

www.tranzlaty.com

Die Nachtigall und die Rose
The Nightingale and The Rose

"Sie sagte, dass sie mit mir tanzen würde, wenn ich ihr rote Rosen brächte"
'She said that she would dance with me if I brought her red roses'
"Aber in meinem ganzen Garten gibt es keine rote Rose!" rief der junge Student
'but in all my garden there is no red rose' cried the young Student
Aus ihrem Nest in der Steineiche hörte ihn die Nachtigall
from her nest in the holm-oak tree the nightingale heard him
und sie schaute durch die Blätter hinaus und wunderte sich
and she looked out through the leaves, and wondered

"Keine rote Rose in meinem ganzen Garten!" rief er
'No red rose in all my garden!' he cried
und seine schönen Augen füllten sich mit Tränen
and his beautiful eyes filled with tears
"Von welchen kleinen Dingen hängt das Glück ab!"
'On what little things does happiness depend!'
"Ich habe alles gelesen, was die Weisen geschrieben haben"
'I have read all that the wise men have written'
"Alle Geheimnisse der Philosophie gehören mir"
'all the secrets of philosophy are mine'
"Doch in Ermangelung einer roten Rose ist mein Leben elend geworden"
'yet for want of a red rose my life is made wretched'

"Hier ist endlich ein wahrer Liebhaber!" sagte die Nachtigall
'Here at last is a true lover' said the nightingale
"Nacht für Nacht habe ich von ihm gesungen, obwohl ich ihn nicht kannte"
'Night after night have I sung of him, though I knew him not'
"Nacht für Nacht habe ich den Sternen seine Geschichte erzählt"
'Night after night have I told his story to the stars'
"Und jetzt sehe ich ihn"
'and now I see him'

"Sein Haar ist so dunkel wie die Hyazinthenblüte"
'His hair is as dark as the hyacinth-blossom'
"Und seine Lippen sind so rot wie die Rose seiner Begierde"
'and his lips are as red as the rose of his desire'
"aber die Leidenschaft hat sein Gesicht wie bleiches Elfenbein gemacht"
'but passion has made his face like pale Ivory'
"Und der Kummer hat ihr Siegel auf seine Stirn gesetzt"
'and sorrow has set her seal upon his brow'

"Der Prinz hat morgen einen Ball veranstaltet," sagte der junge Student
'The Prince has organized a ball tomorrow' said the young student
"Und meine Liebe wird da sein"
'and my love will be there'

"Wenn ich ihr eine rote Rose bringe, wird sie mit mir tanzen"
'If I bring her a red rose, she will dance with me'
"Wenn ich ihr eine rote Rose bringe, werde ich sie in meinen Armen halten"
'If I bring her a red rose, I will hold her in my arms'
"Und sie wird ihren Kopf an meine Schulter lehnen"
'and she will lean her head upon my shoulder'
"Und ihre Hand wird in der meinen gefaltet sein"
'and her hand will be clasped in mine'

"Aber in meinem Garten gibt es keine rote Rose"
'But there is no red rose in my garden'
"so werde ich einsam sitzen"
'so I will sit lonely'
"Und sie wird an mir vorbeigehen"
'and she will go past me'
"Sie wird nicht auf mich achten"
'She will have no heed of me'
"Und mein Herz wird brechen"
'and my heart will break'

"Hier ist der wahre Liebhaber!" sagte die Nachtigall
'Here indeed is the true lover' said the nightingale
"Was ich singe, leidet er"
'What I sing of he suffers'
"Was für mich Freude ist, ist für ihn Schmerz"
'what is joy to me is pain to him'
"Wahrlich, Liebe ist etwas Wunderbares"
'Surely love is a wonderful thing'
"Liebe ist kostbarer als Smaragde"

'love is more precious than emeralds'

"Und die Liebe ist teurer als feine Opale"
'and love is dearer than fine opals'
"Perlen und Granatäpfel können keine Liebe kaufen"
'Pearls and pomegranates cannot buy love'
"Liebe wird auch nicht auf dem Markt verkauft"
'nor is love sold in the market-place'
"Liebe kann man nicht von Händlern kaufen"
'love can not be bought from merchants'
"Auch kann die Liebe nicht auf einer Waage für Gold aufgewogen werden"
'nor can love be weighed on a balance for gold'

"Die Musiker werden auf ihrer Tribüne sitzen", sagte die junge Studentin
'The musicians will sit in their gallery' said the young student
"Und sie werden auf ihren Saiteninstrumenten spielen"
'and they will play upon their stringed instruments'
"Und meine Liebe wird zum Klang der Harfe tanzen"
'and my love will dance to the sound of the harp'
"Und sie wird zum Klang der Geige tanzen"
'and she will dance to the sound of the violin'
"Sie wird so leicht tanzen, dass ihre Füße den Boden nicht berühren"
'She will dance so lightly her feet won't touch the floor'

"Und die Höflinge werden sich um sie drängen"
'and the courtiers will throng round her'
"Aber sie wird nicht mit mir tanzen"

'but she will not dance with me'
"Weil ich keine rote Rose habe, die ich ihr geben könnte"
'because I have no red rose to give her'
Er warf sich ins Gras
he flung himself down on the grass
und er vergrub sein Angesicht in den Händen und weinte
and he buried his face in his hands and wept

"Warum weint er?" fragte eine kleine grüne Eidechse
'Why is he weeping?' asked a little Green Lizard
während er mit dem Schwanz in der Luft vorbeirannte
while he ran past with his tail in the air
"Warum eigentlich?" fragte ein Schmetterling
'Why indeed?' said a Butterfly
während er nach einem Sonnenstrahl umherflatterte
while he was fluttering about after a sunbeam
"Warum eigentlich?" flüsterte ein Gänseblümchen seinem Nachbarn mit leiser, leiser Stimme zu
'Why indeed?' whispered a daisy to his neighbour in a soft, low voice

"Er weint um eine rote Rose," sagte die Nachtigall
'He is weeping for a red rose' said the nightingale
"Für eine rote Rose!?" riefen sie
'For a red rose!?' they exclaimed
"Wie lächerlich!"
'how very ridiculous!'
und die kleine Eidechse, die so etwas wie ein Zyniker war, lachte laut

and the little Lizard, who was something of a cynic, laughed outright

Aber die Nachtigall verstand das Geheimnis des Kummers des Studenten
But the nightingale understood the secret of the student's sorrow
und sie saß schweigend in der Eiche
and she sat silent in the oak-tree
und sie dachte an das Geheimnis der Liebe
and she thought about the mystery of love
Plötzlich breitete sie ihre braunen Flügel aus
Suddenly she spread her brown wings
und sie erhob sich in die Lüfte
and she soared into the air

Sie ging wie ein Schatten durch den Hain
She passed through the grove like a shadow
und wie ein Schatten segelte sie durch den Garten
and like a shadow she sailed across the garden
In der Mitte des Gartens stand ein schöner Rosenstrauch
In the centre of the garden was a beautiful rose-tree
und als sie den Rosenstrauch sah, flog sie zu ihm hinüber
and when she saw the rose-tree, she flew over to it
und sie setzte sich auf einen Zweig
and she perched upon a twig

"Gib mir eine rote Rose!" rief sie
'Give me a red rose' she cried
"Gib mir eine rote Rose und ich werde dir mein süßestes Lied singen"

'give me a red rose and I will sing you my sweetest song'
Aber der Baum schüttelte den Kopf
But the Tree shook its head
"Meine Rosen sind weiß," antwortete der Rosenstrauch
'My roses are white' the rose-tree answered

"So weiß wie der Schaum des Meeres"
'as white as the foam of the sea'
"Und weißer als der Schnee auf dem Berg"
'and whiter than the snow upon the mountain'
"Aber geh zu meinem Bruder, der um die alte Sonnenuhr wächst!"
'But go to my brother who grows round the old sun-dial'
"Vielleicht gibt er dir, was du willst"
'perhaps he will give you what you want'

So flog die Nachtigall zu seinem Bruder hinüber
So the nightingale flew over to his brother
der Rosenstrauch wächst um die alte Sonnenuhr
the rose-tree growing round the old sun-dial
"Gib mir eine rote Rose!" rief sie
'Give me a red rose' she cried
"Gib mir eine rote Rose und ich werde dir mein süßestes Lied singen"
'give me a red rose and I will sing you my sweetest song'
Aber der Rosenstrauch schüttelte den Kopf
But the rose-tree shook its head
"Meine Rosen sind gelb," antwortete der Rosenstrauch
'My roses are yellow' the rose-tree answered

"So gelb wie das Haar einer Meerjungfrau"
'as yellow as the hair of a mermaid'
"Und gelber als die Narzisse, die auf der Wiese blüht"
'and yellower than the daffodil that blooms in the meadow'
"Bevor der Mäher mit seiner Sense kommt"
'before the mower comes with his scythe'
"Aber geh zu meinem Bruder, der unter dem Fenster des Studenten wächst."
'but go to my brother who grows beneath the student's window'
"Und vielleicht gibt er dir, was du willst."
'and perhaps he will give you what you want'

So flog die Nachtigall zu seinem Bruder hinüber
So the nightingale flew over to his brother
Der Rosenstrauch wächst unter dem Fenster des Studenten
the rose-tree growing beneath the student's window
"Gib mir eine rote Rose", rief sie
'give me a red rose' she cried
"Gib mir eine rote Rose und ich werde dir mein süßestes Lied singen"
'give me a red rose and I will sing you my sweetest song'
Aber der Rosenstrauch schüttelte den Kopf
But the rose-tree shook its head

"Meine Rosen sind rot," antwortete der Rosenstrauch
'My roses are red' the rose-tree answered
"So rot wie die Füße der Taube"
'as red as the feet of the dove'
"Und röter als die großen Korallenfächer"

'and redder than the great fans of coral'
"Die Korallen, die sich in der Ozeanhöhle wiegen"
'the corals that sway in the ocean-cavern'

"Aber der Winter hat meine Adern kalt gemacht"
'But the winter has chilled my veins'
"Und der Frost hat meine Knospen erstickt"
'and the frost has nipped my buds'
"Und der Sturm hat meine Zweige zerbrochen"
'and the storm has broken my branches'
"Und ich werde dieses Jahr überhaupt keine Rosen haben"
'and I shall have no roses at all this year'

"Eine rote Rose ist alles, was ich will!" rief die Nachtigall
'One red rose is all I want' cried the nightingale
"Gibt es keinen Weg, wie ich es bekommen kann?"
'Is there no way by which I can get it?'
"Es gibt einen Weg," antwortete der Rosenstrauch.
'There is a way' answered the rose-tree'
"aber es ist so schrecklich, dass ich es dir nicht zu sagen wage"
'but it is so terrible that I dare not tell you'
"Sag es mir!" sagte die Nachtigall
'Tell it to me' said the nightingale
"Ich habe keine Angst"
'I am not afraid'

"Wenn du eine rote Rose willst," sagte der Rosenstrauch
'If you want a red rose' said the rose-tree

"Wenn du eine rote Rose willst, musst du die Rose aus der Musik bauen"
'if you want a red rose you must build the rose out of music'
"Während das Mondlicht auf dich scheint"
'while the moonlight shines upon you'
"Und du sollst die Rose mit deinem eigenen Herzblut beflecken"
'and you must stain the rose with your own heart's blood'

"Du mußt mir mit der Brust gegen den Dorn singen"
'You must sing to me with your breast against a thorn'
"Die ganze Nacht musst du mir vorsingen"
'All night long you must sing to me'
"Der Dorn muss dein Herz durchbohren"
'the thorn must pierce your heart'
"Dein Lebensblut muss in meine Adern fließen"
'your life-blood must flow into my veins'
"Und dein Lebensblut muss mein eigenes werden"
'and your life-blood must become my own'

"Der Tod ist ein hoher Preis für eine rote Rose!" rief die Nachtigall
'Death is a high price to pay for a red rose' cried the nightingale
"Das Leben ist allen sehr lieb"
'life is very dear to all'
"Es ist angenehm, im grünen Wald zu sitzen"
'It is pleasant to sit in the green wood'
"Es ist schön, die Sonne in ihrem goldenen Wagen zu beobachten"
'it is nice to watch the sun in his chariot of gold'

"Und es ist schön, den Mond in seinem Perlenwagen zu beobachten"
'and it is nice to watch the moon in her chariot of pearl'

"Süß ist der Duft des Weißdorns"
'sweet is the scent of the hawthorn'
"Süß sind die Glockenblumen, die sich im Tal verstecken"
'sweet are the bluebells that hide in the valley'
"Und süß ist das Heidekraut, das auf dem Hügel weht"
'and sweet is the heather that blows on the hill'
"Doch die Liebe ist besser als das Leben"
'Yet love is better than life'

"Und was ist das Herz eines Vogels im Vergleich zum Herzen eines Menschen?"
'and what is the heart of a bird compared to the heart of a man?'
So breitete sie ihre braunen Flügel zum Flug aus
So she spread her brown wings for flight
und sie erhob sich in die Lüfte
and she soared into the air
Wie ein Schatten fegte sie über den Garten
She swept over the garden like a shadow
und wie ein Schatten segelte sie durch den Hain
and like a shadow she sailed through the grove

Der junge Student lag noch im Garten
The young Student was still lying in the garden
und seine Tränen waren noch nicht getrocknet in seinen schönen Augen

and his tears were not yet dry in his beautiful eyes
"Sei glücklich!" rief die Nachtigall
'Be happy' cried the nightingale
"Du sollst deine rote Rose haben"
'you shall have your red rose'
"Ich werde deine Rose aus Musik machen"
'I will make your rose out of music'
"Während das Mondlicht auf mich scheint"
'while the moonlight shines upon me'

"Und ich werde deine Rose mit dem Blut meines Herzens beflecken"
'and I will stain your rose with my own heart's blood'
"Alles, was ich im Gegenzug von dir verlange, ist, dass du ein wahrer Liebhaber sein wirst"
'All that I ask of you in return is that you will be a true lover'
"weil die Liebe weiser ist als die Philosophie, obwohl sie weise ist"
'because love is wiser than Philosophy, though she is wise'
"Und die Liebe ist mächtiger als die Macht, obwohl er mächtig ist"
'and love is mightier than power, though he is mighty'

"Flammenfarben sind seine Flügel"
'flame-coloured are his wings'
"Und gefärbt wie Flamme ist sein Leib"
'and coloured like flame is his body'
"Seine Lippen sind süß wie Honig"
'His lips are as sweet as honey'
"Und sein Atem ist wie Weihrauch"
'and his breath is like frankincense'

Der Student blickte vom Gras auf
The Student looked up from the grass
und er lauschte der Nachtigall
and he listened to the nightingale
aber er konnte nicht verstehen, was sie sagte
but he could not understand what she was saying
denn er wusste nur, was er in Büchern gelesen hatte
because he only knew what he had read in books
Aber die Eiche verstand, und er wurde traurig
But the Oak-tree understood, and he felt sad

Er mochte die kleine Nachtigall sehr
he was very fond of the little nightingale
weil sie ihr Nest in seinen Zweigen gebaut hatte
because she had built her nest in his branches
"Singe ein letztes Lied für mich", flüsterte er
'Sing one last song for me' he whispered
"Ich werde mich sehr einsam fühlen, wenn du fort bist"
'I shall feel very lonely when you are gone'
Da sang die Nachtigall der Eiche
So the nightingale sang to the Oak-tree
und ihre Stimme war wie Wasser, das aus einem silbernen Krug sprudelte
and her voice was like water bubbling from a silver jar

Als sie ihr Lied beendet hatte, stand die Studentin auf
When she had finished her song the student got up
und er zog ein Notizbuch hervor
and he pulled out a note-book
und er fand einen Bleistift in seiner Tasche
and he found a lead-pencil in his pocket

›Sie hat Form‹, sagte er zu sich selbst
'She has form' he said to himself
"Dass sie Gestalt hat, kann ihr nicht abgesprochen werden"
'that she has form cannot be denied to her'
"Aber hat sie Gefühl?"
'but does she have feeling?'
"Ich fürchte, sie hat kein Gefühl"
'I am afraid she has no feeling'

"Eigentlich ist sie wie die meisten Künstler"
'In fact, she is like most artists'
"Sie ist ganz Stil, ohne jede Aufrichtigkeit"
'she is all style, without any sincerity'
"Sie würde sich nicht für andere opfern"
'She would not sacrifice herself for others'
"Sie denkt nur an Musik"
'She thinks merely of music'
"Und jeder weiß, dass die Kunst egoistisch ist"
'and everybody knows that the arts are selfish'

"Trotzdem muss man zugeben, dass sie einige schöne Noten hat"
'Still, it must be admitted that she has some beautiful notes'
"Schade, dass ihr Lied nichts bedeutet"
'it's a pity her song does not mean anything'
"Und es ist schade, dass ihr Lied nicht nützlich ist"
'and it's a pity her song is not useful'
Und er ging in sein Zimmer
And he went into his room
und er legte sich auf sein Bettchen

and he lay down on his little pallet-bed
und er fing an, an seine Liebe zu denken, bis er einschlief
and he began to think of his love until he fell asleep

Und als der Mond am Himmel schien, flog die Nachtigall zum Rosenstrauch
And when the moon shone in the heavens the nightingale flew to the Rose-tree
und sie lehnte ihre Brust an den Dorn
and she set her breast against the thorn
Die ganze Nacht sang sie mit der Brust gegen den Dorn
All night long she sang with her breast against the thorn
und der kalte Kristallmond beugte sich herab und lauschte
and the cold crystal Moon leaned down and listened
Die ganze Nacht sang sie
All night long she sang
und der Dorn drang tiefer und tiefer in ihre Brust ein
and the thorn went deeper and deeper into her breast
und ihr Lebensblut verebbte von ihr
and her life-blood ebbed away from her

Zuerst sang sie von der Geburt der Liebe im Herzen eines Jungen und eines Mädchens
First she sang of the birth of love in the heart of a boy and a girl
Und auf dem obersten Zweig des Rosenstrauches blühte eine herrliche Rose
And on the topmost branch of the rose-tree there blossomed a marvellous rose

Blütenblatt folgte auf Blütenblatt, als Lied auf Lied folgte
petal followed petal, as song followed song
Zuerst war die Rose noch blass
At first the rose was still pale

so bleich wie der Nebel, der über dem Fluss hängt
as pale as the mist that hangs over the river
so bleich wie die Füße des Morgens
as pale as the feet of the morning
und so silbern wie die Flügel der Morgenröte
and as silver as the wings of dawn
So bleich der Schatten einer Rose in einem silbernen Spiegel
As pale the shadow of a rose in a mirror of silver
so bleich wie der Schatten einer Rose in einem Wasserbecken
as pale as the shadow of a rose in a pool of water

Aber der Baum rief der Nachtigall zu;
But the Tree cried to the nightingale;
"Drücke dich näher, kleine Nachtigall, oder es kommt der Tag, ehe die Rose fertig ist."
'Press closer, little nightingale, or the day will come before the rose is finished'
Da drückte sich die Nachtigall fester an den Dorn
So the nightingale pressed closer against the thorn
und ihr Lied wurde lauter und lauter
and her song grew louder and louder
denn sie sang von der Geburt der Leidenschaft in der Seele eines Mannes und einer Magd

because she sang of the birth of passion in the soul of a man and a maid

Und die Blätter der Rose färbten sich zartrosa
And the leaves of the rose flushed a delicate pink
wie die Röte im Gesicht des Bräutigams, wenn er die Lippen der Braut küsst
like the flush in the face of the bridegroom when he kisses the lips of the bride
Aber der Dorn hatte ihr Herz noch nicht erreicht
But the thorn had not yet reached her heart
So blieb das Herz der Rose weiß
so the rose's heart remained white
denn nur das Blut einer Nachtigall kann das Herz einer Rose färben
because only a nightingale's blood can crimson the heart of a rose

Und der Baum rief der Nachtigall zu;
And the Tree cried to the nightingale;
"Drücke dich näher, kleine Nachtigall, oder es kommt der Tag, ehe die Rose fertig ist."
'Press closer, little nightingale, or the day will come before the rose is finished'
Da drückte sich die Nachtigall fester an den Dorn
So the nightingale pressed closer against the thorn
und der Dorn berührte ihr Herz
and the thorn touched her heart
und ein heftiger Schmerz durchzuckte sie
and a fierce pang of pain shot through her

Bitter, bitter war der Schmerz
Bitter, bitter was the pain
und wilder und wilder wuchs ihr Lied
and wilder and wilder grew her song
weil sie von der Liebe sang, die durch den Tod vollendet wird
because she sang of the love that is perfected by death
Sie sang von der Liebe, die im Leben nicht stirbt
she sang of the love that does not die in life
Sie sang von der Liebe, die nicht im Grab stirbt
she sang of the love that does not die in the tomb
Und die wunderbare Rose wurde purpurrot wie die Rose des östlichen Himmels
And the marvellous rose became crimson like the rose of the eastern sky
Purpurrot war der Gürtel aus Blütenblättern
Crimson was the girdle of petals
Purpurrot wie ein Rubin war das Herz
as crimson as a ruby was the heart

Aber die Stimme der Nachtigall wurde schwächer
But the nightingale's voice grew fainter
und ihre kleinen Flügel fingen an zu schlagen
and her little wings began to beat
und ein Film kam über ihre Augen
and a film came over her eyes
Schwächer und schwächer wurde ihr Gesang
fainter and fainter grew her song
und sie fühlte, wie etwas sie in ihrer Kehle würgte
and she felt something choking her in her throat
Dann gab sie einen letzten Musikstoß von sich

then she gave one last burst of music

der weiße Mond hörte es, und sie vergaß die Morgenröte
the white Moon heard it, and she forgot the dawn
und sie verweilte am Himmel
and she lingered in the sky
Die rote Rose hörte es
The red rose heard it
und die Rose zitterte vor Ekstase
and the rose trembled with ecstasy
und die Rose öffnete ihre Blütenblätter der kalten Morgenluft
and the rose opened its petals to the cold morning air

Echo trug es zu ihrer violetten Höhle in den Hügeln
Echo carried it to her purple cavern in the hills
und es weckte die schlafenden Hirten aus ihren Träumen
and it woke the sleeping shepherds from their dreams
Er schwamm durch das Schilf des Flusses
It floated through the reeds of the river
und die Flüsse trugen ihre Botschaft bis zum Meer
and the rivers carried its message to the sea

"Sieh, sieh!" rief der Baum
'Look, look!' cried the Tree
"Die Rose ist jetzt fertig"
'the rose is finished now'
Aber die Nachtigall gab keine Antwort
but the nightingale made no answer
denn sie lag tot im hohen Grase, mit dem Dorn im Herzen

for she was lying dead in the long grass, with the thorn in her heart

Und gegen Mittag öffnete der Student sein Fenster und schaute hinaus
And at noon the student opened his window and looked out
"Was für ein wunderbares Glück! Er weinte
'What a wonderful piece of luck! he cried
"Hier ist eine rote Rose!"
'here is a red rose!'
"So eine Rose habe ich noch nie gesehen"
'I have never seen any rose like it'
"Es ist so schön, dass ich sicher bin, dass es einen langen lateinischen Namen hat"
'It is so beautiful that I am sure it has a long Latin name'
Er beugte sich vor und pflückte die Rose
he leaned down and plucked the rose
Dann lief er mit der Rose in der Hand zum Haus des Professors
then he ran up to the professor's house with the rose in his hand

Die Tochter des Professors saß in der Tür
The professor's daughter was sitting in the doorway
sie wickelte blaue Seide auf eine Spule
she was winding blue silk on a reel
und ihr kleiner Hund lag zu ihren Füßen
and her little dog was lying at her feet
"Du sagtest, du würdest mit mir tanzen, wenn ich dir eine rote Rose brächte"

'You said that you would dance with me if I brought you a red rose'
"Hier ist die röteste Rose der Welt"
'Here is the reddest rose in all the world'
"Du wirst es heute Abend tragen, als nächstes dein Herz"
'You will wear it tonight, next your heart'
"Während wir zusammen tanzen, wird es dir sagen, wie sehr ich dich liebe"
'While we dance together it will tell you how I love you'

Aber das Mädchen runzelte die Stirn
But the girl frowned
"Ich fürchte, es passt nicht zu meinem Kleid"
'I am afraid it will not go with my dress'
"Wie auch immer, der Neffe des Kammerherrn hat mir einige echte Juwelen geschickt"
'Anyway, the Chamberlain's nephew sent me some real jewels'
"Und jeder weiß, dass Juwelen mehr kosten als Blumen"
'and everybody knows jewels cost more than flowers'
"Nun, Sie sind sehr undankbar!" sagte der Student ärgerlich
'Well, you are very ungrateful!' said the Student angrily
und er warf die Rose auf die Straße
and he threw the rose into the street
und die Rose fiel in die Gosse
and the rose fell into the gutter
und ein Wagenrad lief über die Rose
and a cart-wheel ran over the rose

"Undankbar!" sagte das Mädchen
'Ungrateful!' said the girl
"Lass mich dir das sagen; Du bist sehr unhöflich"
'Let me tell you this; you are very rude'
"Und wer bist du überhaupt? Nur ein Student!"
'and who are you anyway? Only a Student!'
"Du hast nicht einmal silberne Schnallen an deinen Schuhen"
'You don't even have silver buckles on your shoes'
"Der Neffe des Kammerherrn hat viel schönere Schuhe"
'The Chamberlain's nephew has far nicer shoes'
Und sie erhob sich von ihrem Stuhl und ging ins Haus
and she got up from her chair and went into the house

"Was für ein dummes Ding die Liebe ist!" sagte der Student, während er fortging
'What a silly thing Love is' said the Student, while he walked away
"Liebe ist nicht halb so nützlich wie Logik"
'love is not half as useful as Logic'
"Weil es nichts beweist"
'because it does not prove anything'
"Die Liebe erzählt immer von Dingen, die nicht passieren werden"
'Love always tells of things that won't happen'
"Und die Liebe lässt dich Dinge glauben, die nicht wahr sind"
'and love makes you believe things that are not true'
"In der Tat ist die Liebe ziemlich unpraktisch"
'In fact, love is quite unpractical'

"In der heutigen Zeit ist es wichtig, praktisch zu sein"
'in this age being practical is everything'
"Ich werde zur Philosophie zurückkehren und Metaphysik studieren"
'I shall go back to Philosophy and I will study Metaphysics'
Also kehrte er in sein Zimmer zurück
So he returned to his room
und er zog ein großes, verstaubtes Buch hervor
and he pulled out a great dusty book
und er fing an zu lesen
and he began to read

Das Ende / The End

www.tranzlaty.com

www.ingramcontent.com/pod-product-compliance
Lightning Source LLC
Chambersburg PA
CBHW020133130526
44590CB00040B/618